A DAY
THE LIFE OF
AN ENGINE
DRIVER

ANTHONY DAWSON

AMBERLEY

First published 2018

Amberley Publishing
The Hill, Stroud,
Gloucestershire, GL5 4EP

www.amberley-books.com

ISBN: 978 1 4456 6922 9 (print)
ISBN: 978 1 4456 6923 6 (ebook)

British Library Cataloguing in Publication Data.
A catalogue record for this book is available from the British Library.

Typeset in 10pt on 13pt Celeste.
Typesetting by Amberley Publishing.
Printed in the UK.

Contents

Introduction

'I noticed the driver turning handles, and making it go, and thought to myself it would be a fine thing to be an engine-driver, and have the control of a wonderful machine like that.' – Charles Dickens, *Mugby Junction* (1866).

Until the demise of main line steam on the British railways in 1968, it was said that almost every little boy wanted to grow up to be an engine driver. Even today, fifty years later, that is a dream which many still cherish and can fulfil thanks to the growth of the heritage railway industry. Starting with the Tal-Y-Llyn Railway in 1951, as of 2016 there were around 130 heritage railway and tramways in the UK, representing some 550 route miles, and an estimated £250 million to the leisure economy.[1] They provide an opportunity for a largely volunteer work force (approximately 20,000 in 2016) to fulfil their childhood dream of working on a steam railway, either as a cleaner, fireman, driver, or even as a guard or signalman. These are careers that, unlike in steam days, are open to all with the passion and time for steam. While there is undoubtedly a glamour and mystique to steam, the locomotives require hard, dirty, physical graft. Training methods have remained largely unchanged since the demise of main line steam, with it still taking years of hard work and diligent study to move up from being a cleaner to a driver.

The purpose of this book is twofold: to educate and to entertain, giving a taste of what life is like at 'the mucky end' of a day out on a heritage railway to those 'on the cushions', and to inspire others to pick up the shovel, paraffin and rags.

---

1 https://www.citymetric.com/transport/britains-heritage-railways-are-booming-demographic-timebomb-looms-1801

CHAPTER 1

Preparation

The preparation of a steam locomotive for the road is a time-honoured ritual as old as main line railways themselves; the routine of lighting the fire, oiling round, and cleaning was familiar to the first group of main line railwaymen who worked on the Liverpool & Manchester Railway in 1830. Indeed, today's engine (Great Western Railway Pannier Tank No. 7714) is little different – other than in size and complexity – to Robert Stephenson's *Planet* of 100 years earlier, featuring a multi-tubular boiler with a smokebox (containing a blast pipe) and chimney at the front end; a firebox within the boiler barrel at the opposite; and inside cylinders (under the smokebox) driving a crank axle. In fact, Bill Holmes (who drove *Planet* all those years ago) would probably recognise much of her layout and technology.

Bridgnorth station (viewed from 'Pan Pudding Hill') in an Edwardian colour postcard.

The main entrance of Bridgnorth station.

Most heritage railways have sleeping accommodation for volunteers; those on the Severn Valley are provided by converted BR Mark 1s, but a new accommodation block is being built.

Looking down the full length of Platform 1 at Bridgnorth.

The dawn chorus wakes me before my alarm tweets at 06.45. Time for a quick mug of coffee (one of those instant ring-pull, self-heating jobbies), wash and brush up before going on shed. There's a slight nip in the air, making me glad of the serge of my Victorian LNWR firing jacket (but I'll regret it later as the day warms up). The station cat yawns languidly from the footbridge, stretches and pads off in search of breakfast.

Bridgnorth station on the Severn Valley Railway nestles alongside the river, at the foot of a great mount, on which the shattered keep of Bridgnorth Castle juts like a snaggletooth at the crazy angle of 15 degrees off the vertical (three times that of the Leaning Tower of Pisa!). The line was opened in 1862, connecting Hartlebury with Shrewsbury, via Stourport-on-Severn, Bewdley, Hampton Loade, Bridgnorth, Coalport, Iron Bridge and Berrington. After 101 years, it was closed to passengers in 1963, and to freight in 1969. The line was progressively re-opened from 1974, culminating with the opening of the new Kidderminster Town railway station in 1984.

It's just gone 07.00 on a beautiful May morning when we sign on to our turn in the little Victorian cottage which serves as Bridgnorth's yard office. Our train is due off Bridgnorth at 10.40, so that gives us more than enough time to get the engine (and ourselves) ready for the day ahead. In GWR days, forty-five minutes was allowed for the preparation of a small engine such as No. 7714, but many firemen would often book on earlier, giving themselves an hour.

At Bridgnorth Motive Power Depot, GWR heavy freight locomotive No. 2857 and Bulleid 'West Country' No. 34027 *Taw Valley* bask in the sun.

Left: Little and large: *Taw Valley* and No. 7714.

Below: This week's engine: GWR Pannier Tank No. 7714. (Gareth C. Price)

Having read the day's notices, signed the requisite paperwork and collected the engine logbook, we make our way over to today's engine, No. 7714, which is one of a batch of twenty-five 57XX Class engines built by Kerr, Stuart of Stoke-on-Trent in 1930 for the Great Western Railway to a design produced by Charles Collet, the Chief Mechanical Engineer of the GWR in 1928. The design was so successful that 863 of them were built in various batches between 1929 and 1950. Some sixteen have been preserved, including a second example (No. 5764) at the Severn Valley, which is a genuine GWR product, having been built at Swindon in 1929. No. 7714 can be identified as a non-Swindon product through having visible rivets on the water tanks. It is rumoured that the Kerr, Stuart 57XXs were better than those built by the GWR at Swindon, but GWR aficionados dispute this. She worked for the GWR/BR Western Region until 1959, when she was sold to the National Coal Board to work at Penallta Colliery in South Wales. No. 7714 was rescued by members of the Severn Valley Railway in 1973, and following a lengthy restoration entered service in 1992, but was withdrawn 'out of ticket' in 2009. Work to return her to steam commenced in 2012, and was completed in November 2016. Like the little 14XX, the Pannier Tank is a 'classic' GWR tank engine, found on hundreds of branch lines working short passenger trains (some were auto-fitted), working trip goods, or shunting in yards. Generations of children will be familiar with them through *Duck the Great Western Engine* from the Thomas series of books by the Reverend Awdry.

No Swindon product she: No. 7714's works plate proudly proclaims 'Kerr, Stuart & Co. Ltd. Stoke-on-Trent.'

Valley Panniers: Nos 7714 and 5764 at Kidderminster Town. (Gareth C. Price)

Pannier Tank No. 1935 was built at Wolverhampton Works in 1884 and was based at Oxford Depot, and latterly Birkenhead. She was withdrawn in 1953.

Above and below: Panniers doing what they do best – working short trip-goods in the Oxford area during the 1930s.

Today's crew consists of Dave Ward, who is our booked driver, Mike Ward, who is our booked fireman, and Tom Mills, who is in the final stages of his training before qualifying as 'Passed Cleaner', which is a cleaner who is passed to fire locomotives, but who is awaiting a vacancy on the fireman roster. Both Mike and Dave Ward are 'Passed Firemen', which means that they are firemen who are qualified to drive, but are awaiting a driver vacancy on the main roster. Dave also drives on the 'big railway'. Tom is responsible for lighting-up, cleaning and shunting. He is a very welcome extra pair of hands, which makes the workload easier and the crew's week more enjoyable as a result. The fourth, unofficial member of the team is your scribe, who is also a 'Passed Cleaner' (but on a different heritage railway, and qualifications are not necessarily always transferable).

The rostering of crews and 'turns' is another part of railway life that is as old as the railways. Nowadays it can be done online using HOPS software, but from the earliest days of the Liverpool & Manchester, large blackboards were located in the running sheds (and in sheds ever since):

> With letters corresponding to the days of the week; opposite to which, for each day, is set a mark, if the man is at work, or absent ... On the time-boards is noted down on what engine or engines each man has been engaged, and their duty, and the result of each board is entered into a book, daily.

Such boards were used right up to the end of main line steam and are still used on many preserved railways. Indeed, the whole 'Link System' of promotion goes back to the old Liverpool & Manchester and the earliest days.

Didcot Railway Centre provides an atmospheric recreation of a GWR main line depot. 14XX Class No. 1466 stands over the pit.

Western tank engines on parade: Pannier Tanks Nos 3650 and 3733 stand in company with 56XX Class No. 6697 at Didcot. (Gareth C. Price)

Fire and Water

Before the fire can be laid and lit, the fireman has to make sure that there is water in the boiler. He does this by using the single gauge glass on the left-hand side (or fireman's side) of the cab. The gauge glass consists of a toughened glass tube which straddles the water level of the boiler, providing a quick visual guide as to how much water is in the boiler. The 'bottom nut' is usually an inch or so above the top, or 'crown sheet', of the firebox, so that when no water is showing in the glass, there will be (hopefully) a minimal amount of water over the crown sheet. If the crown sheet becomes uncovered, without the water around the firebox drawing away the fierce heat of the fire there is a likelihood that it will overheat and collapse as it is made from copper, which melts at 1,085 degrees, and the heat of the fire can be twice that. Screwed into the top of the crown sheet is an early warning device known as a 'fusible plug'. This was an invention of Richard Trevithick, and consists of a bronze bush with a lead core. If the water level drops too low, and the crown sheet overheats, then the lead core will melt before the copper. With the lead core melted, high-pressure steam will jet into the firebox and warn the crew that the water level is dangerously low. If this happens, the feed water must be put on and the firebox doors kept closed. When safe, the fire can be dropped.

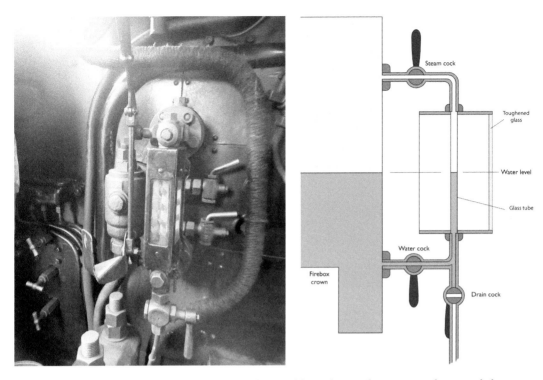

Above left: No. 7714's water gauge and test cocks; visible is the single operating lever and the drain cock.

Above right: How a traditional water gauge works. The one on No. 7714 works on the same principle, although the operating handles are a bit different. (Andrew Mason)

Gauge glasses have two valves, or 'cocks': the top cock controls the admission of steam, and the lower controls water. The glass tube has protector (called a 'gauge frame') and a striped refractor plate behind the tube makes the water level easier to see; the diagonal stripes are reversed when viewed through the water. There is also a drain valve, and this is opened to allow the gauge glass to be drained and blown through to remove any sediment or dirt which make cause a blockage and therefore a false reading. On older engines, both cocks are controlled individually, but No. 7714 has them controlled by a single lever, which, when the glass tube bursts, is much quicker (and therefore safer) to isolate. The water level should be kept in the top third of the glass, and a 'weather eye' kept on the water level in the boiler, with the feed used periodically to top up the water as it is used. Similarly, the water level will fluctuate whether the engine is going uphill (giving a high reading) or downhill (low reading), and water should be especially topped up with the latter to keep the crown sheet covered. As a failsafe, most engines have two gauge glasses, but on the Great Western it was usual for there to be a single gauge glass and a pair of test cocks.

Firemen are always trained to be able to change a gauge glass. Harold Gasson, a GWR fireman in the 1940s, recalled that his driver deliberately removed the gauge frame and smashed the gauge glass, not only to get him used to the experience, but also to show him how to change a tube in an emergency:

Joe ... enquired if I had ever change a gauge glass .... Then to my horror Joe took off the gauge frame and calmly smashed the glass with a spanner. The result was almost indescribable as steam and water roared into the cab. I felt for the gauge frame handle, found it and shut off the steam by pulling it down, then lifted the blow-through cock. At last there was peace in the cab, with Joe sitting on his seat taking a pinch of snuff and making comments on what a nice fine day it was to learn how to change a gauge glass. I was never worried about a gauge glass breaking again.

Having made sure there is water in the boiler, the firebox has to be inspected. The ends of the tubes, stay-heads and rivet heads are checked to make sure there are no leaks, that the tubes are clear and that the fusible plug is intact. Similarly, any wash-out plugs and mud-hole doors on the outer firebox are inspected for any signs of leakage. The fire bars are also checked to make sure that they are clear of any clinker or ashes and that they are intact and have not burned through. No. 7714 has a rocking grate and a hopper ashpan (see Chapter 3), which makes it quicker and easier to clear the grate than a traditional locomotive with traditional cast-iron firebars and flat-bottomed ashpan below. No. 7714 was fitted with a rocking grate and hopper ashpan as an in-preservation modification to make servicing the locomotive at the end of the day easier.

This morning, our fireman cleans out the remains of last night's warming fire, which was put in to keep the engine warm to reduce (or at least mitigate) the damage caused by the heating-cooling thermal cycle a boiler will pass through, and also to reduce the time taken to raise steam in the morning ready for duty.

Above left: Tom drapes a dust sheet over the smokebox apron and footplating ...

Above right: ... opens the smokebox door ...

Above left: ... shovels out the char to the waiting wheelbarrow ...

Above right: ... and brushes clean the smokebox door ring.

At the opposite end of the boiler, the smokebox has to be emptied of char and ashes. This is done in the morning when the engine is relatively cold to prevent the tube plate being damaged from cold air rushing into a hot smokebox and boiler and chilling them, leading to thermal stresses. A wheelbarrow, shovel, brush and dust sheet are collected. The dust sheet is spread out on the smokebox apron. The smokebox door darts are unfastened, and ashes cascade onto the dust sheet as the door is gently opened, which are then shovelled into the wheelbarrow; the spark-arrester is cleaned and the rim and inside of the smokebox door are brushed clean of any remaining ashes or dust which would prevent it from making an air-tight seal when closed, and from maintaining a proper vacuum. This vacuum is an important part of the function of a locomotive boiler: the blast pipe (which exhausts used steam from the cylinders into the smokebox) creates a vacuum in the smoke box, which draws the hot air and combustion products from the fire through the boiler tubes. If this vacuum is poor or destroyed by a leaking smokebox door, then the engine will not steam well and unburned combustion products could ignite in the smokebox, which can burn the paint off the smokebox and at worst warp and damage the smokebox itself.

Cleaners and Steam Raisers

In the days of main line steam, the fireman would sign on duty to find all of this work already done for him by a steam raiser, with the boiler and bunker already full and the fire lit and banked up. On some larger preserved railways steam raisers are usually still appointed during the very busy summer months. Being a steam raiser was a step up from being a cleaner.

Adrian Bailey began work at Gorton Tank near Manchester in 1961 aged seventeen, with an ambition to become an engine driver. Thanks to an uncle who was a platelayer and welder, he secured an interview and a position as a cleaner at the Tank. Gorton had been built back in the 1840s by Richard Peacock, who was the first locomotive superintendent of what would later grow to be the Great Central Railway and was the other half of the famous Gorton engine-builders, Beyer, Peacock & Co. Adrian's experience was as follows:

> You started at the bottom and worked your way up. It was the best way to learn. I was issued overalls and then taken to the sheds, where I was shown how to clean engines by ex-drivers who for health reasons could no longer drive trains.
>
> This involved lots of rags and wadding (the sort of stuff used in soft furnishings) and cleaning the side rods and eccentrics, smoke boxes, smokebox door, number plates and nameplates, engine cab backplates and face plates, cab floor and checking all the essentials, i.e. brush, lamp, spanners, bucket, a tin of twelve detonators (and made sure they were all in date), and two red flags.
>
> Having spent a few months as a cleaner I was then moved up to training as a fireman. There was a group of five of us. You booked on with the steam raiser, who were ex-drivers doing depot work. The steam raiser was there to show you how to light the fire, and teach you about the boiler. I was initially lighting-up the engine: loading the firebox with coal and timber, and lighting it with oily rags. Steam raisers also had to fill the water tank and make sure there was enough coal in the tender for the journey. A lot of the engines when you were steam raising had already been worked on by fitters, and after coming out of the fitting shop were like new, and we'd take them out on test. Others had been with the boiler smiths, who'd drained the water out of the boilers in boiler cleaning, and you had to put fresh water in.

After three months, Adrian went to on to the Pilot Link, which was covered by drivers who, for health reasons, were not allowed to work on the main line but were still permitted to drive in the yard. He had the relatively easy task of firing the pilot engine, making up trains and shunting in the yards at Ardwick, Ashburys and Guide Bridge, and taking out the engineer's train with its special saloon, which they 'used to inspect the track. It was laid out with a big table, and proper chairs, and carpeting. One end was all glass so they could observe the track.' From the Pilot Link the next promotion was to the Goods Link on the various 'Trip Jobs' between different yards. Having become a 'Passed Cleaner', it was a case of waiting until there was a vacancy in the roster for regular firemen in the Freight Link and then the Passenger Link, and from there to 'Passed Fireman'.

Each depot had its own way of working; but with Gorton closing, Adrian made an '8C Move' from Gorton to Newton Heath – which was one of the last steam depots in the country. Newton Heath had been opened by the Lancashire & Yorkshire Railway in 1877, and the following year founded a football team, which today is known as Manchester United. At Newton Heath, he had to start again from the bottom.

When you booked on as fireman, you found out who your driver was. You had ten minutes to book on and twenty minutes to book off. You got your docket for working, read all the notices, if there were any speed restrictions or track work. Each office had a supervisor and a time keeper and runners. We always dealt with them, you didn't always see the Depot Managers, as they were always in their offices. We did see the Divisional Manager for Manchester, who was based at Piccadilly. He liked drivers and firemen and would travel round, get a footplate ride to see what was going on and how everyone was, and he knew who you were, too.

After booking on we had to go to stores to get the tools we needed; you had to make sure you got all your tools at prep otherwise it could be very embarrassing on the road. Newton Heath couldn't compare with Gorton; Gorton was very particular. Everything had to be spotlessly clean and was: the lamps, buckets, spanners, detonators, everything was clean, tidy and sorted out, and up to a point the engines were clean. At Newton Heath, everything was filthy; on loco prep, you had to slack it all down before you started work.

Many of the drivers Adrian fired to were characters, including one who wore with his slops a white collar and tie, gloves, and bulled boots, and could get off an engine as clean as when he got on!

When you got in a link, you had the same driver from week to week, month to month – annual leave excepting. If you had a good driver, you'd get on like a house on fire. If he knew you, he'd know what you, as a fireman, were capable of; and you knew what he was like as a driver. You almost had to be a mind-reader. So that you got the experience, the good drivers would let you have a drive. It was the only way to learn. Some drivers would just work the engine off the regulator, and never think of notching up; put it in full forward gear and keep it there. Which made the life of the fireman that much harder. On the Eastern Region the fireboxes were long and narrow, with a small oval firehole door with this little flap. The shovel had a long narrow blade, so you could get it into the back corners, but you couldn't get big lumps of coal through, so some firemen opened the main door. There was a real knack to getting the coal to the front of the 'box. On a Black Five you had sliding doors, worked by a lever, which was much easier to use. You had to be careful with the safety valves of a B1 if the station had a glass roof. Unlike a Black Five, they gave you no indication they were about to lift. The valves would lift water too and soak passengers on the platform.

Adrian remembered that promotion between different BR regions often varied, so that on the London Midland there was often little in the way of an age gap between firemen and drivers, but on the Eastern the driver was usually much older than the fireman. During his time on steam, Adrian worked on former Great Central 'Pom Poms' and 'Tinies', LNER B1s (there were two at Gorton: No. 61011 *Waterbuck* and No. 61013 *Reedbuck*), Midland 3Fs and 4Fs, LMS 8F and also Black Fives: 'Beautiful engines. They'd steam like a kettle and do anything you asked of them.' He also fired No. 70013 *Oliver Cromwell* on various Blackpool Club Specials from Manchester to Blackpool, and also fired on Bulmer's Cider Specials to York. Many celebrities of the day were regular passengers on the Blackpool trips and they always had to run to time. The Blackpool runs allowed plenty of time for the engine crews to enjoy themselves, too:

We'd turn the engine and put it in the siding. Put a big fire under the door, make sure the boiler was full and tied up the engine. The time was yours till night time when we made the run back, so we'd go for a jar and get pie and chips.

Until BR published its 'Black Book' in 1957, there had been very little in the way of official learning material for aspiring drivers; one of the most popular pre-1957 publications had first been published in 1908. Throughout the Victorian period, the lack of training material and formal qualifications resulted in Locomotive Superintendents like Michael Reynolds of the LBSCR leading a virtually single-handed crusade to improve the training of footplate crews. Bowen Cook of the LNWR and Harry Ivatt on the Great Northern produced their own books in the late 1800s, but training was (and is) still on the job, supplemented by Mutual Improvement Classes. It takes time and experience to learn to fire and drive a steam locomotive, and many heritage railways run MICs for the benefit of their working members, and often share resources and examples of 'best practice' with each other. The 'Black Book' still remains the most comprehensive and intelligible book on the subject.

Cleaning an engine can be a physically demanding, but satisfying job. Paintwork is gone over with de-greaser (usually a mix of diesel and paraffin), scrapers and rags to remove the worst of the muck and grease before polishing with neat paraffin – one rag to put on, one to take off and polish up. Brightwork is cleaned with good old 'Brasso' or 'Peak Polish.' In Victorian days, brick dust and oil was used for brightwork, and an engine's plate work would be cleaned and then given a coat of tallow or wax, which could be polished to a shine or into different patterns. Although this looked very smart, it had one major drawback, and that was dust. Tallow especially would remain slightly sticky, and by the end of the day an engine would be filthy. It would all need to be scraped off, cleaned, and applied again. The tools of the trade remain unchanged since the end of main line steam, comprising bundles of rags, paraffin and elbow grease.

Training to be a driver on a preserved railway in 2018 is little changed from Adrian's time in 1961, or even Bill Holmes' day in 1830. The whole system of promotion from cleaner to fireman to driver was worked out nearly 200 years ago by the Liverpool & Manchester:

In appointing firemen, it was desirable to look forward to their becoming enginemen, and with this in view it must be an advantage to a man to have been employed in a fitter's shop. The Directors wished, therefore, that the firemen should be supplied from the cleaners and the repairing sheds.

While the old Liverpool & Manchester preferred literate men on their footplates, Brunel famously believed that literacy was not only unimportant, but was in fact an impediment! During Adrian's time at Gorton Tank, he only had four months to learn to be a fireman, but it would generally take several years to pass from cleaner to Passed Cleaner (who could fire an engine in the yard and go on short trip workings) before getting a regular turn as fireman, starting first on goods trains and then progressing to passenger workings. Then it would be learning to drive, becoming a Passed Fireman in the process. Even on heritage railways, training is on-the-job hard work, taking several years to learn the art, the craft, of firing an engine. There isn't a 'fast track' to firing or driving an engine other than through time spent learning on the job. Cleaners had to be young and fit, to be

Plenty of elbow grease, paraffin and rags are needed to help make No. 7714 look her best.

able to scramble up between the frames of an engine to clean the big ends and eccentrics, and to clean the inside of the frame: outside valve gear made this both safer and easier. They often found themselves doing a plethora of other dirty jobs, such as 'coaling and watering, fire lighting, emptying smokeboxes, helping with boiler wash outs and all the other dirty, filthy jobs with steam engines'. LMS driver Laurie Earl recalled that in his youth (on the LNWR) the engine cleaners even did all the laundry and washing for the men of their depot! While cleaning a hot firebox in summer could be torture, akin to being in a sauna, in winter it was certainly a 'perk' in the warm, where a crafty cigarette could be smoked, too. No one seemed to notice that fireboxes took longer to clean in winter than in summer.

Making Steam

With the locomotive safe to light-up, a barrow full of old dry wood can be collected, together with dirty, oily rags. The remainder of last night's warming fire is rocked through the grate into the ashpan. Northumbrian steam coal is shovelled in a thin layer evenly across the grate. Bits of broken timber are then stacked on top. Finally, an oily rag is wrapped around a long, straight piece of timber and set alight. It's thrust into the firebox, and the timber soon catches. It's followed by two more. Thick, black, oily smoke begins to curl from the chimney.

Above left: Dry wood is collected for lighting-up.

Above right: The remains of last night's warming fire is rocked through the grate.

Below left: A layer of coal is spread across the grate before dry timber is placed on top.

Below right: Oily rags are set alight and thrust into the firebox.

Where there's smoke, there's fire. No. 7714 starts to raise steam.

With the boiler prepped, the driver now carries out his own inspection of the engine. A 'Not to be Moved' board is put in the front buffer beam. It does exactly what it says on the tin – the engine is not to be moved as there is someone underneath. Mike has collected rags, a bottle of lubricating oil and an oil can from the oil store and goes under the engine. In the twenty-first century the driver goes under with a battery torch – usually a Bardic Lamp – but in the days of main line steam he would have lit his way with a guttering flare lamp. Here, he is looking at all the fixings (nuts, cotters, split pins) to make sure they are all secure, and the leaf springs to ensure no leaf has broken. He takes out the cork stoppers from each of the oil pots on the axle box 'underkeeps' and pours thick lubricating oil into each. Hot water dribbles from the cylinder drain cocks and runs down my neck; even for one of somewhat Hobbit-esque stature, there's not much room under here. Mike works methodically, making his way to the back of the engine. Springs and underkeeps done, he now tops up the oil pots for the bottom slide of the slide bars. Next, he has to oil up the 'big ends' and cranks. The 'big end' is, as the name suggests, the bigger of the two ends of the connecting rod which connects the piston rod to the crank. Mike has to squeeze up in the small gap between the front of the firebox and the crank throws and eccentrics in order to get to the oiling points. This done, he wriggles free, and then makes sure the underkeeps of the trailing axle (behind the firebox) are well oiled.

Above: Leading wheel springs and axle-box underkeeps, which need to be inspected and lubricated.

Right: Looking up (from under the cylinder block) to the 'small end', slide bars and eccentric rods.

Left: No. 7714's 'big end' and crank throws.

Below: Mike has to squeeze up between the crank throws and firebox to lubricate the eccentrics and big ends.

Attending to the axle-box underkeeps on the trailing wheels.

He now turns his attention to the other oiling points of the motion. On a 57XX Class, this is a form of 'Stephenson Link' valve gear. He has to clamber between the boiler, running plate and motion to get to them. The lubricator of the vacuum pump is also topped up. Finally, the feed boxes for the axle boxes get topped up, as do the oil pots on the outside coupling rods. I follow Mike around, wiping off spilled oil and muck from yesterday.

With the fire lit and burning well and the engine oiled up, we go round and clean the plate work, footplating, wheels and rods. It's important to do this to prevent any dirt and grit from getting on any bearing surfaces, or damaging the paint finish, but also to make the engine look good for the passengers as part of their day out. It's about pride in the job, and all loco crews take great pride in having a clean engine. I dry brush and wash off any remaining dust and ash (left over from ashing out the smokebox) from the running boards, before giving them a polish and rub up with paraffin and rags. The coupling rods and wheels receive the same treatment. The inside of the cab will get a wipe down and a polish with paraffin, too. Keeping on top of the cleaning like this makes it easier further down the line, and stops the engine from getting filthy. It also makes a clean and safe working environment for the loco crew. In Victorian times on the LNWR, an engine was not allowed out on to the road unless it had passed a literal white glove inspection by the Shed Foreman!

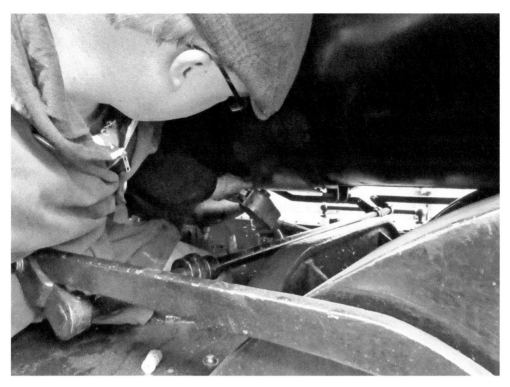

Above and below: Mike has to clamber between the frames and boiler to attend to the oiling-points on the valve gear.

Right: Lubricating the vacuum pump ...

Below left: ... coupling rods ...

Below right: ... and filling the axle box oil boxes.

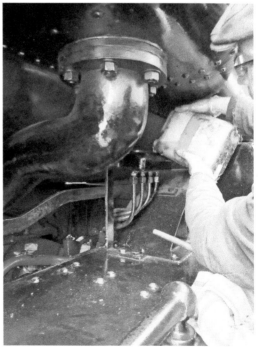

In the cab, Tom is keeping an eye on his fire. Once the wood has burned through and the whole grate is alight, more coal can be added, keeping the fire packed in the back corners and in a saucer shape all around the box, so that it is thin in the middle and thick around the sides where it comes into contact with the firebox walls. Once the first pressure is raised the blower can be put on to draw the fire. The blower is a perforated ring that sits

Left: Tom attends to his fire, shovelling coal into the fiery heart of the engine.

Below: Around us, other locomotives are coming to life, raising steam.

A driver's eye view of the road ahead.

close to the top of the blast pipe nozzle and is fed with live steam from the boiler. It works in the same way as the blast pipe, by creating an artificial draught in the smokebox, which draws the combustion products from the fire through the boiler tubes, making the fire burn hotter. As the boiler pressure beings to rise, so the blower becomes harder, and needs trimming back occasionally. When 100 psi is reached both injectors can be tested to make sure both are working and we can put water back into the boiler. With the fitness to run examination completed, we can come off shed.

Coal and Water

Examination complete, and once tea has been drunk and sufficient boiler pressure has been raised to move No. 7714, Dave takes her forward to the watering and coaling point. With a warning shriek from her whistle she moves forward in first valve, shrouded in white mist from her open drain cocks, clattering through the station approach so that we can change road. Tom jumps down to change the points and we back down to the water column. Tom climbs up on top of the tank to open the filler cap and swings round the arm and Mike works the water valve to fill up No. 7714's water tanks, slung either side of the boiler. The tanks are capable of holding 1,200 gallons of water between them, and they are joined via a 'balance pipe', which keeps the water level equal in both tanks. Under the cast-iron arm of the water column is a brazier with a long chimney, which is used in winter months to prevent the water from freezing. On hot, sunny days in the summer months it's always a good idea to keep the tanks topped up – because the tanks are slung alongside

Above: The GWR water crane and 'devil' (to stop the water freezing) at Bridgnorth.

Left: Tom clambers onto the tank top to open the filler while Mike works the water valve.

the boiler, the water gets heated, and hot sunshine can also warm up the water in the tank. The combined effect can warm the water so much that the injectors (which put water back into the boiler) can become temperamental. Adrian Bailey remembered how: 'Some of the steam drivers were comical. They would *never* pass a water column without filling up, despite knowing where, and how far, they were going.'

Tanks full, we need something to boil all that water with – coal. In GWR days it would have been Welsh steam coal, but today we're burning Northumbrian hard coal. It is hard and quick to ignite and burn, but is smoky. In comparison, Welsh steam coal is soft and slow burning (with a tendency to 'cauliflower' as it does so), and because of its high carbon content is relatively smoke free. The coal bunker of No. 7714 can hold 3 tons 6 cwt of coal and, in the twenty-first-century version of a coal stage, a JCB digger is used to tip three bucketfuls of coal into the bunker, avoiding the back-breaking labour of coaling by hand using buckets.

With brimming tanks, a full bunker and a good head of steam, we can come off shed and back down onto our train on Platform 1.

A more traditional method of coaling up: the coaling stage at Didcot.

Above left and right: Coaling up is greatly facilitated through modern, mechanical means.

Below: Drain cocks blowing, No. 7714 moves off yard to go and pick up her train.

CHAPTER 2

A Quick Cab Tour

The parish church clock chimes 10 a.m. as No. 7714 is backed onto her train. Tom climbs down and 'goes in between' in the dangerous position between the engine and carriages. Before he can go between, he needs permission from the driver that it is safe to do so, that the train and locomotive are secure. He climbs down and back on the same side each time, and informs the driver when he is out from between the vehicles, in a safe position. He shackles her on and connects the vacuum hoses; there's no need for the steam heat pipes today. With the engine coupled and piped-up, a full brake test is carried out: Dave creates a full 25 inches

Backing down on to her train at Bridgnorth.

Above: Today's train, comprising 'blood and custard' BR Mark 1s.

Below left and right: Tom climbs down between the locomotive and carriage to shackle on and connect the vacuum hoses.

vacuum, and then destroys it. The guard walks the length of the train to checks the blocks are on. He then takes the back bag off its dummy, gives the hand signal 'create vacuum' to Dave (who does so) in order to check for continuity. This done, he then puts the bag back on its dummy. Finally, the guard walks the length of the train, checking blocks are off, and confirms that the brake test was successful so that the train is safe to go out on the road.

There's now an opportunity for tea and breakfast. Dave does himself proud, delivering foot-long baguettes with bacon, sausage and scrambled egg. No. 7714's safety valves begin to feather – they're allowed to lift once to make sure that they lift at the proper pressure – as we sip scalding hot tea, enjoying our breakfast, and field questions from interested passengers about the engine and also about our snap, usually along the lines of 'Is it true you cook on the engine?', 'Do you cook to order?' or 'Err! I wouldn't eat that!' There is a knack to cooking your breakfast on the shovel, usually heating the shovel in the fire and placing it on the fire door ring and using it as a frying pan. While sausages, bacon and burgers, and even steak are relatively easy, I have yet to successfully do eggs. Occasionally, culinary disasters can occur. In one instance, the former Railway Officer at MOSI during one busy half term holiday heated up a tin of all day breakfast and forgot to pierce the lid of the tin ... and the rest of the day was spent picking up pieces of mushroom or sausage from the engine. In order to stop flames and smoke blowing back into the cab when the fire door is open, the blower must be put on, but not too hard. For example, while heating some miniature snack-size pork pies on the shovel for lunch one firing turn on *Agecroft No. 1*, the blower was on a bit too hard. The pies were sucked off the shovel, and one of them whiffled through a boiler tube, was ejected out of the chimney, and the charred remains drifted past the cab window. What the members of the public must have thought about three grown men coming off the footplate in hysterics and quoting lines from the Goons' 'The Dreaded Batter-Pudding Hurler of Bexhill-on-Sea' is unknown. Breakfast over, we can wash up and get into clean gear for the footplate; usually a flat cap and a blue denim firing jacket and trousers, or a bib and brace.

Cab Controls: Fireman's Side

Before we move off, perhaps it is best to describe the controls of No. 7714. George Jackson Churchward, the Chief Mechanical Engineer of the GWR, standardised cabs of his engines, not just within each class, but across his entire locomotive fleet. This means that the controls of No. 7714 are, if not in exactly the same place as those in a 'King' or 'Castle' class engine, or a tiny 14XX, then at least recognisable.

We will start on the fireman's side of the footplate. The fireman is responsible for the safe management of the boiler, ensuring that there is always sufficient water in the boiler; that there is always steam when the driver needs it; and that the boiler is not wasting water and fuel by blowing off through the safety valve (10 gallons of water a minute can be lost through excessive blowing off).

To allow him to put water in the boiler, Tom uses a device called an injector, invented by the Frenchman Hénri Giffard in 1855 for the steam boiler of his dirigible. The Manchester company Sharp, Stewart & Co. purchased the first licence in Britain to produce Giffard injectors, but they were very slow to catch on, only gradually replacing water pumps by the 1870s.

No. 7714's cab. A: 'Mason' or steam-heat reducing valve; B: steam heat steam supply; C: whistle chains; D: blower; E: water gauge; F: injector steam supplies; G: driver's combined steam and vacuum brake control; H: regulator handle.

There are various types of injector, but those on No. 7714 are of the 'simple' type, which are gravity fed and use live steam to work them. An injector uses a series of cones to operate: a steam cone; a combining cone; and a delivery cone. Steam is admitted to the injector using a valve on the steam manifold in the cab. The water supply from the tank is also controlled by a lever on the footplate, which can be worked with a deft flick of the toe. Steam is admitted at boiler pressure and passes through the first cone, the steam cone, and this changes the pressure energy of the steam to velocity energy. In the second, or combining cone, the slowly moving stream of water meets the fast moving jet of steam from the first cone. The cooler feed water condenses the steam (which is why it is important that the feed water in the tank is as cold as possible, to make sure the steam fully condenses to water), resulting in a jet of water that jumps the overflow gap between the combining cone and the delivery cone. The delivery cone converts the velocity energy of the combined jet into pressure energy so that

Right: No. 7714's fireman's side injector.

Below: The working of a simple injector. (Andrew Mason)

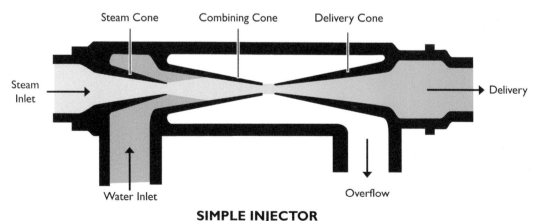

SIMPLE INJECTOR

Above left: On the fireman's side is an oil box for the trailing axle; test cocks for the water tank (to check the water level); and the injector water valve.

Above right: Water gauge, test cocks and clack box.

it can overcome the boiler pressure, which is keeping the non-return valve (called a clack valve) shut. Water is then injected into the boiler, with the injector making its distinctive singing noise. It sounds very complicated, but in fact it is relatively simple. That said, injectors can be temperamental beasts.

At head height the fireman has two gauges: that on the left is for the steam heating for the carriages, while that on the right is the boiler pressure gauge. Tom needs to keep the boiler pressure between 180 psi and 200 psi (when the boiler blows off); if the pressure drops below around 160 psi, the engine becomes sluggish and does not respond well. To keep the boiler pressure up, Tom needs to fire using the old mantra 'a little and often', methodically placing between six and eight shovelfuls of coal on the fire, as well as keeping a weather eye on his water gauge.

Coiled around the fireman's seat is the slacker pipe, which is fed from the injector. This is used to wash down the footplate to keep it clean and tidy, as well as to slack down the coal in the bunker – which is especially important when running bunker first with a tank engine in order to keep dust to a minimum. He will slack down the footplate and coal several times throughout each run to Kidderminster and back.

To control the flow of primary air to the fire, Tom has access to damper levers, which open and shut the dampers under the firebox. Due to the risk of lineside fires during the summer months, the dampers are not used during this part of the year, so instead the fire is managed using the blower, the firehole doors and the drop-down air flap in order

Boiler pressure gauge (right) and steam heat pressure gauge (left). The fireman wants to keep the boiler pressure between 180 and 190 psi.

to regulate the amount of secondary air that passes into the firebox through the firehole. To direct this flow of air onto the burning coal there is a deflector plate mounted above the firehole door. This is there to ensure that sufficient oxygen reaches the coal fire so that all the volatile matter (mostly hydrocarbons) is properly burned to prevent smoke. There is also a brick arch in the firebox. This is the clever invention of Matthew Kirtley, which enables locomotives to burn coal without making smoke. The law used to state engines had to 'consume their own smoke', so coke, a relatively smokeless fuel, was the more expensive fuel of choice. The brick arch slows down the speed at which the combustion products leave the firebox, meaning that the volatile matter does not make smoke and is properly burned.

A quick glance at the chimney will tell the fireman how well his fire is burning. If there is thick black smoke, then that suggests all the volatile matter from the fire has not been properly burned as there is not enough air, or too much coal has been put on in one go. If there is no smoke at all other than a heat haze, then that suggests there is too much air. What is wanted is very light grey smoke at the chimney mouth, showing that the volatile matter is being properly burned (to get maximum heat from the coal), and that no heat is being lost either from incomplete combustion or the combustion products passing through the boiler too quickly and going to waste.

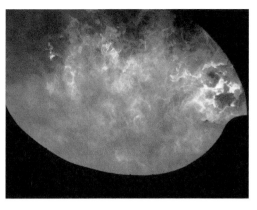

Above: The incandescent mass at the heart of No. 7714.

Left: The fireman's tool of the trade: a shovel and coal.

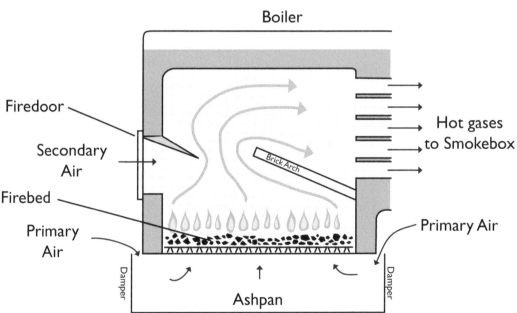

Primary air flow is through the bed of the fire (and controlled via the dampers); while secondary air, through the firehole door, is directed onto the fire via the baffle plate and controlled with adept use of the flap and firebox doors. The brick arch slows the flow of combustion products through the firebox so that the volatile matter can be properly burned. (Andrew Mason)

Above left: Controlling the air flow through the fire: doors open and flap up ...

Above right: ... flap down and doors half open ...

Right: ... and doors nearly closed.

Tom keeps the fire well packed under the firehole door, thick around the sides and thin in the middle.

Although the controls for the steam heat gear and steam supply for the fireman's side injector are on his side of the cab, the blower valve is actually on the driver's side.

There are few hard and fast rules about firing an engine on the move. When to fire, depending on steam requirements, comes from experience: from learning the route with an experienced driver and fireman, and learning when and where you have to fire and when you don't. It takes time, experience, and aptitude to make a good fireman. It's either something you're good at and 'get' almost straight away, or you will struggle with; poor firing can result in waste of fuel and water, or lack of steam leading to loss of time and delays. A good fireman is perfectly in tune with his engine, in an almost symbiotic relationship with her; with both man and machine in perfect harmony. He knows her moods as well as he knows his own; he knows the road and when he needs to make steam and when he can take a breather. To watch Tom in action is poetry in motion.

Driver's Side

The driver is responsible for the safe working of the engine and the safety of her crew. To be able to walk across the footplate from the fireman's side takes years of hard graft and practical experience. The best main line 'Top Link' men who drove the crack expresses were men with forty years of railway work behind them, often in their sixties; Joseph

Duddington, who drove *Mallard* on her record-breaking 126 mph run in 1938, was sixty-one and retired aged sixty-seven. A driver, especially the 'Top Link' express man, was someone everybody looked up to, because they knew it had taken them a lifetime of work to get to the pinnacle of their career.

The most obvious of the driver's controls are the red-painted regulator and the reversing lever. The regulator lever opens and closes the regulator valve, which admits the steam to the cylinders. On No. 7714 it is a double-beat regulator, which means that it has a first (or pilot) valve and a second, larger, main valve. The pilot valve is used when shuffling around the yard at low speed, while the main valve is the main running valve.

The reversing lever, via the Stephenson link valve gear, controls both the direction of travel and also the 'cut off'. By this, we mean the moment during the stroke of the piston in the cylinder that the admission of steam is 'cut off', i.e. stopped, and the point at which the exhaust port is opened. The sooner the steam is cut off in the cylinder, the more the steam will work expansively; in other words, it will continue to expand in the cylinder to push the piston. This makes an engine more economical to run as it uses less steam. Opening the exhaust port slightly sooner reduces what is termed 'back pressure' in the cylinder from the steam remaining from the previous stroke. By reducing the back pressure, a freer

Above left: The red-painted regulator handle, which controls the pilot and main valve. It works anti-clockwise, so the driver pulls upwards to open it.

Above right: The reversing lever, in mid-gear. Push forward for fore-gear, and backward for back-gear. The graduated quadrant allows the driver to control the valve gear 'cut off' in order to use steam expansively.

exhaust is obtained, and thus a freer running engine. Because No. 7714 uses traditional 'slide valves' and has a relatively high boiler pressure of 200 psi, the driver has to shut off before he can notch up or down: shutting off relieves the valves of pressure, making them easier to move.

In front of the driver is the combined vacuum and steam brake control, which simultaneously controls the steam brake on the engine and the vacuum brakes on the carriages (or fitted wagons). The vacuum is created using a device called an ejector (which works rather like an injector). It took many years – and, sadly, several severe accidents – for Britain's railways to finally fit continuous automatic brakes to its trains, the disaster at Armagh in June 1889 being the tipping point, with public opinion and politicians overruling many of the private railway companies who objected to the fitting of such brakes on the grounds of cost. By continuous we mean every vehicle in the train is braked, and by automatic that such brakes are instantaneous in operation, and will come into operation even if the train is separated. Although the train involved in the Armagh disaster had continuous brakes, they were not automatic and did not work when part of the train separated.

On the engine, the 'large ejector' is used to create the vacuum to release the brakes, and make brake applications, while the air pump is used while running to exhaust any air that might have leaked into the train pipe in order to maintain the vacuum. The use of a pump on smaller engines was a frugal move by the GWR as it saved on steam that would be

Above left: The driver's combined steam and vacuum brake control, which simultaneously applies the steam brake on the engine and vacuum brakes on the train.

Above right: The brake duplex vacuum gauge, giving the vacuum in the train pipe and reservoir. A vacuum of 21 inches is needed to keep the brakes off.

used by a small ejector, and therefore coal. The tish-tock of the vacuum pump on No. 7714 becomes as familiar as the ticking of a grandfather clock.

There is a continuous pipe running the full length of the train; where vehicles meet, flexible rubber hoses looking rather like elephant's trunks are used. These pipes can be connected and disconnected to allow vehicles to be added or removed from the train, and it is important that the pipes must be sealed to maintain the vacuum. If at any point a coupling breaks, causing the train to separate, the hoses will also separate, meaning the vacuum is destroyed and the brakes are automatically applied.

Under every carriage, or fitted wagon, is a brake cylinder containing a piston, which then connects via mechanical linkages to the brake gear, which works the brake blocks. To release the brakes, a vacuum is created that causes the piston in the brake cylinder to fall to the bottom. In order to apply the brake, the vacuum in the train pipe is reduced, which creates a pressure differential in the brake cylinder, causing the piston to rise because the air pressure beneath the piston is higher than that above it. The pressure of this vacuum is measured in inches of mercury (Hg). While the BR standard was a vacuum of 21 inches Hg, that on the Great Western (they always liked to be different) was 25 inches Hg, which meant that there was more force available for braking. While at first glance this difference

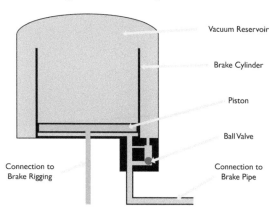

Vacuum Reservoir

Brake Cylinder

Piston

Ball Valve

Connection to
Brake Rigging

Connection to
Brake Pipe

Vacuum Brake Cylinder - Brake Released

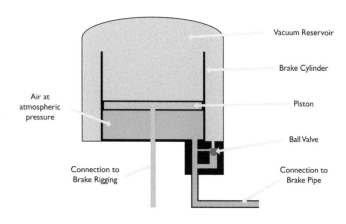

Vacuum Reservoir

Brake Cylinder

Air at
atmospheric
pressure

Piston

Ball Valve

Connection to
Brake Rigging

Connection to
Brake Pipe

The working of a vacuum brake: a vacuum is created by the engine, which causes the piston in the brake cylinder to fall, releasing the brakes. As soon as this vacuum is destroyed, air at atmospheric pressure rushes under the piston, forcing it up, to apply the brakes. (Andrew Mason)

Vacuum Brake Cylinder - Brake Applied

may appear to present problems when a locomotive only capable of producing 21 inches Hg is coupled to former GWR stock, this is overcome thanks to the vacuum relief valve (also called a 'pepper pot' valve from its distinctive brass cover). If a GWR locomotive comes in with a train of GWR coaches and an ex-LMS locomotive is then put on the train, the strings are pulled on the coaches to destroy the vacuum; the brakes come off at 21 inches thanks to the pepper pot valve, which keeps the vacuum at 21 inches, irrespective of the loco coupled to the train.

The driver's control valve has three positions: the left-hand side is to blow off or create vacuum, and uses the large ejector; the middle is the running position; and the right-hand side is to apply the brake, which applies both the vacuum brakes on the train and the steam brake on the engine. When running light engine or loose-coupled goods trains, it is only used to apply the engine brakes as there is no vacuum brake available. The driver needs to take care to pause momentarily between applying and releasing the brakes, in order to exhaust the steam brake while on the road.

Also prominent is the sight feed lubricator, which feeds thick steam oil down to the pistons and slide valves. Although it looks complicated with its row of valves and sight glasses, it is fairly simple in operation, working on the principle that oil floats on water. It is a form of displacement lubricator; steam condenses under pressure and the oil rises and is forced down the main steam pipe by the steam pressure. This is called hydrostatic lubrication. With a sight feed lubricator, steam pressure is used to provide a constant

The sight feed lubricator, which controls the supply of oil to the pistons and valves.

supply of oil to the pistons and valves. The oil is subjected to steam under boiler pressure, and is atomised through a very fine nozzle into the sight glass feeds, which are filled with water. These droplets of oil then float on the water and are displaced into the steam pipe. By adjusting the oil and steam valves, the amount of oil delivered to the pistons and cylinders can be finely controlled.

Mounted on the cab side sheet, with its obvious brass warning bell, is the ATC, or Automatic Train Control system. This is an early form of train protection system developed by the GWR as long ago as 1906. It was designed to give warning when a train was approaching a Distant signal (we'll talk more about signals later), and, if the warning signal was ignored, would automatically apply the brakes. There were two audible warnings: a siren, which would sound if a signal to stop was ahead, instructing the driver to be prepared to stop at the appropriate 'Stop' signal; and the ringing of a bell, which meant 'all clear'.

Underneath each engine was a metal skate, and between the rails, about 400 yards from the appropriate signal, was a metal ramp, about 40 feet long. An electric telegraph wire connected the ramp to the Distant signal arm it was protecting. When the signal arm was moved to the 'Off' position ('Proceed'), the ramp was energised via an electric battery, and when the signal is 'On' ('Proceed with caution, and be prepared to stop at the next signal'), the ramp is de-energised.

Driver's side Automatic Train Control apparatus, which warns the driver if a signal to stop is head.

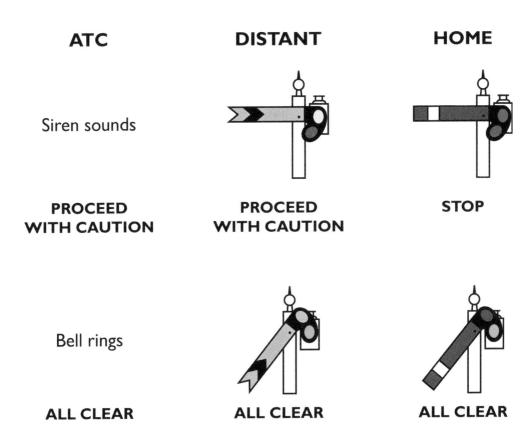

ATC	DISTANT	HOME
Siren sounds		
PROCEED WITH CAUTION	**PROCEED WITH CAUTION**	**STOP**
Bell rings		
ALL CLEAR	**ALL CLEAR**	**ALL CLEAR**

GWR signalling and ATC: when a Home signal is 'On' (danger), that warning is repeated by the Distant ('proceed with caution and be prepared to stop at the next signal') and the ATC siren sounds. If the Home signal is 'Off' (proceed), then the Distant will also be 'Off' and the ATC bell will ring. (Andrew Mason)

As the locomotive passes over the ramp, the skate is lifted and operates a switch on the engine. If the Distant signal is 'On' ('Proceed with caution'), the ramp is de-energised, and when the skate passes over the ramp, the siren will sound and the brakes apply automatically unless the driver quickly cancels the application. But if the Distant signal is 'Off' ('Proceed'), the ramp is energised, and when the skate passes over, the current causes the bell to ring (the siren doesn't sound), without any brake application. This means that if there were any failure in the electrical system, the ramp would be de-energised, so that the brakes would be applied and the siren would sound in the cab.

Up near the cab roof are two whistle chains – one for the higher-pitched engine whistle and the second for the lower-pitched guard's whistle (they're about an interval of a fifth apart) to signal to the guard of an unfitted freight train to put his brakes on.

Signals and Tokens

The Severn Valley Railway has perhaps the best signalling arrangement of any preserved railway, using traditional semaphore signals. Unlike the vast majority of other railway companies, the Great Western – and later the Western Region – used what are known as 'lower quadrant' signals. This means that when the signal is set at 'danger', the arm is horizontal, and falls to an angle of 45 degrees for 'proceed'. As the signal arm moves, so too do a pair of coloured glass lenses, showing red for 'danger' and green for 'all clear'. Other railway companies (and regions) used 'upper quadrant' signals, so that the arm was still horizontal at 'danger' but it moved up for 'all clear'. Before 1876 most signals were of the lower quadrant type, but an accident on the Great Northern Railway at Abbots Ripton on the night of 21 January 1876, revealed the fatal flaw of such a signal. The weight of snow and ice had forced the signal arm down from the 'danger' to 'all clear' position, which resulted in the 'Special Scotch Express' (called the 'Flying Scotsman' after 1923) colliding, at speed, with a coal train. A second train then ran into the wreckage. Thirteen lives were lost and fifty-three persons were injured. A Court of Inquiry recommended that lower quadrant signals be abandoned and that the default position for all signals be 'danger' rather than 'clear', and that the colour lenses be changed from white and red ('all clear'/'danger') to green and red, so that if a lens broke it did not give a false indication of safety. The Inquiry also provided guidance about the provision of continuous automatic brakes. Sadly, the Board of Trade had no legal powers to enforce these recommendations, but many companies did change their signalling to 'upper quadrant' type; the Great Northern adopted a signal known as a 'somersault', which meant it was difficult for an accumulation of snow or ice to affect the balance of the signal arm.

There are two principal types of signal: Distant and Home. Home or Starter signals are usually placed to control a block, and are essentially stop signals. Their signal arms are painted red (facing the direction of travel) and their spectacle lenses are green (proceed)

Above left: The platform-mounted Starter at Arley.

Above right: The signal gantry at Bewdley, carrying Home, Distant and 'calling on' signal arms.

and red (danger). If a Home signal is 'Off' (proceed), a train may enter that block, but when they are 'On' ('danger') a train cannot enter the block; it must be brought safely to a stand and must not pass the signal. Most stations would have two Home signals: one protecting the entrance to the block, usually termed the Home, and a second controlling the exit, called a Starter.

Distant signals give the driver an advanced warning of the state of upcoming signals, and are usually positioned several hundred yards ahead of the Home they protect. Their signal arms are painted yellow facing the direction of travel and are usually swallow-tailed. At night, the spectacle lenses are yellow (caution) and green (proceed). If a Home signal is 'On' (danger), the Distant will also be 'On' and show caution informing the driver that the next signal is set to Danger and that they must 'proceed with caution'. If the Home is 'Off' (proceed), the Distant will repeat the signal, and also show 'proceed.' Because signal posts are positioned on the left-hand side of the track, but Great Western engines are right-hand drive, it is the job of the fireman to keep a good look-out for the approaching signals.

Tom keeps a good look-out ahead to observe the state of approaching signals.

Tokens, Single Line Working

The Severn Valley Railway (SVR) is only single track, which means it has to be worked bi-directionally. To prevent collisions, it is worked using the 'Absolute Block' method: the line is divided into different 'blocks' (usually via signal boxes at each of the stations) into which only one train may enter and travel at any one time. In order to control this, the Electric Train Token system is used.

A token instrument is installed in the signal box at each end of the single line section, forming an electrically connected pair. Only one token at any one time can be removed from an instrument, and this can only be done with the cooperation of the signalman at the other end of the section. This means that no other token can be removed until the originally removed token has been replaced in one of the two instruments. Possession of the token means that the driver of a train can enter the block controlled by the two signal boxes. He is given the token before entering the block and must give it up when he leaves.

The SVR is divided into two long sections (Bridgnorth and Bewdley North) and two short sections (Hampton Loade and Arley). This means that the SVR can be run with a combination of long and short sections. Hampton Loade and Arley are only switched in according to traffic needs, in order to save on staff, as can the Bridgnorth to Highley and Highley to Bewdley North token sections. Shorter sections are used according to what has been switched in. The token for each section is a different colour – one colour per section (red, yellow, blue or green) – and to prevent tokens being placed into the wrong instrument, each has a set of 'wards' rather like a mortice lock key, which means only the correct token will fit the instrument.

The system works like this: the signalman at box 'A' sends the bell code 'Call Attention' to the signalman at box 'B' to alert them that he is ready to dispatch a train into the section.

Tom prepares to catch the token as we roll into Arley, arm outstretched.

Above: The signalman holds out the token...

Below: ... and Tom's caught it.

When signalman B has received this, he will acknowledge. Signalman A then sends the code 'Is the line clear?' If it is, Signalman B will send the code that it is and accepts the train into his section. If Signalman B accepts the train, they will respond by repeating the bell code, but, on the final beat of the bell code, will keep the bell plunger held in. Keeping the plunger held in releases the mechanism of Signalman A's token instrument, so that, if no other token is presently withdrawn from either instrument, the signalman can remove a token. As Signalman A withdraws the token from their instrument, both signalmen will set the indicators on their instruments to show that a token is out, and in which direction the train is travelling.

Removing the token will unlock the section signal, and this allows the trains to enter the section between the two signal boxes. Signalman A will clear this signal, put the token into a token carrier, and give it to the footplate crew. As a further means of ensuring safety, the fireman (who usually receives the token) will read out loud the signal box names for the single line section they are to pass over. As the train departs, Signalman A will check it is showing the correct tail lamp at the end of the train – which shows that the train is complete and has not divided en route – and send the bell code 'Train Entering Section' to Signalman B.

When the train arrives at the far end of the section the crew will hand the token, in its carrier, to Signalman B. When signalman B has seen the tail lamp on the back of the train or the guard has confirmed the train has arrived complete, Signalman B will place the token in their instrument, put their indicator to normal, and send 'Train Out Of Section' to Signalman A. Signalman A will then return their indicator to normal. These train movements will be recorded by both signalmen using indelible black ink in their Train Register.

A different method is in use between Bewdley South and Kidderminster Town. This uses 'Acceptance Levers', without the use of Electric Train Tokens. The system relies on the track being Track Circuited throughout. Permission for trains to enter the section is given by the use of the special Acceptance Lever, which releases the signal allowing a train to enter the section. The lever is locked when a train is detected – via the Track Circuit – in the section, which prevents it from being pulled to release the signal to allow another train into the section. It also prevents the lever from being returned to the 'normal' position once a train has been accepted into, and is travelling in, the section. This system also prevents trains from entering the section from the opposite direction.

Chapter 3

Out on the Line

Bridgnorth–Hampton Loade

Before we depart, Mike puts eight shovelfuls of coal onto the fire. The fireman should never fire when the train is starting away, and should either do it immediately before departure or wait a little way until the driver has 'notched up'. This is because the temperature of the firebed and brick arch is relatively low before the engine starts moving and the blast pulls the fire. A cool fire and brick arch would mean that the volatile matter in the coal will not burn properly, leading to the production of black smoke, which is something we don't

Mike builds up the fire before departure.

want. When starting away, the firehole door should be closed so that primary air is drawn through the fire to raise the temperature of the firebed.

The starter drops giving permission to proceed, but we can't depart until we have received the token, which gives us the authority to enter the section. In fact, the signalman cannot give us the token until the signal has been cleared, in order to minimise incident risk. We're handed the token for the Bridgnorth–Hampton Loade section: Tom shows it to Dave to confirm we have permission to enter that section. The guard shows his green flag and blows his whistle; we respond with our own whistle. Tom gives the 'right away' and with 180 psi on the clock, Dave puts No. 7714 into full forward gear and joggles open her regulator. Her front end is enveloped in a white cloud from her open drain cocks, and away we go. Dave shuts off briefly so he can bring her reverser back three notches to about 35 per cent (so that steam is admitted for only 35 per cent of the stroke of the piston: for the remaining 65 per cent, the steam is being worked expansively), and No. 7714's exhaust softens as we chatter away from Bridgnorth. It's downhill from Bridgnorth to the viaduct. As we leave the section of continuous welded rail, No. 7714 starts the bounce so characteristic of her class, which is a result of the combination of leaf and coil springs. Pannier crews developed sea legs in order to accommodate the bounce and roll. Thankfully she has wooden floorboards, which prove far easier on the feet and ankles than a steel footplate.

We cross onto the lofty, five-arch Oldbury Viaduct and pass over the main road (the A458). The line immediately to the south of the viaduct was damaged during the 2007 storm.

Above left: Heading out of Bridgnorth.

Above right: Looking back down the train, and into Bridgnorth MPD.

Left: Passing over Oldbury Viaduct, looking down onto Daniels Mill, which has the largest cast-iron mill wheel in England.

Below: An Edwardian postcard, labelled the 'Mill in the Hole'; Daniels Mill can be glimpsed through the centre arch.

3303 MILL IN THE HOLE BRIDGNORTH

On our left is Daniels Mill, which has the largest cast-iron water wheel in England at 38 feet in diameter, and was made in 1854 at Coalbrookdale. The mill dates back to at least the fifteenth century, when it was known as 'Donynges' or 'Dunnings' Mill. The mill ceased working following the death of the last miller in 1957. It was sensitively restored in the late 1950s, and again in 2007–08. Just passing the Mill the feed is put on, and we get an all clear and run straight through Eardington, sounding our whistle in warning at the SW board as the platform at Eardington is a little unsighted around the curve. The River Severn runs alongside in the bottom of the valley; sheep and lambs in the neighbouring fields munch lazily as we pass. On the approach to Hampton Loade, the Distant is against us, but the peg drops and we make our way into Hampton Loade where we have a nine-minute breather.

We run into Hampton Loade at 10 mph, and we drop off the token. Tom leans out over the cab side with the token ready to do the quick change; because we're waiting for another train to come out of section, we hand back our token and can only proceed into the next section once the next section is clear, but it is currently occupied by the approaching train. Once we've received the token for the next section, which is being carried by the approaching train, we can continue our journey. No other train can be on the single as long as we have the token. It is our security that we are the only train on that section at that time.

Coming into the platform, the fireman looks back, counting the carriages into the platform so that the driver knows where and when to stop – one fireman reputedly informed the driver: 'Right, stop alongside that cow in the field.' We pull up at 11.02 and climb down from the cab and to get a breath of fresh air.

Hampton Loade is the home of the Victorian six-wheeler 'Barry Coach', built in 1895. It was found being used as a holiday home just under a century later, in 1992, and is undergoing a lengthy restoration, which it is hoped will be completed in 2020. Hampton Loade is also home to the Paddock Garden Railway. We're held at Hampton Loade until the first train from Kidderminster crosses us, which is headed by No. 1501. She is the only

Our first calling point is Hampton Loade. The lovingly restored buildings are on Platform 1, on the Down side (heading toward Bridgnorth). The platforms can only hold four coaches. (Chris McKenna (Thryduulf, Creative Commons Attribution-Share Alike 4.0 International))

Above: We have a nine-minute wait at Hampton Loade, and take a breather to escape the heat of the cab.

Left: No. 1501 heads bunker-first into Hampton Loade; we will exchange tokens so we can continue our journey to Kidderminster Town.

surviving example of the GWR 15XX Class of Pannier Tanks designed by Hawksworth, with shorter tanks and outside Walschaerts valve gears, of which only ten were built. No. 1501 was built at Swindon in 1949 and worked empty coaching stock movements. She was passed to the NCB in 1961 and was saved for preservation in 1969 by members of the Severn Valley Railway. As she brings her train in, we climb back up into the cab and prepare to depart, getting off at 11.10.

Hampton Loade–Highley

Being in possession of the token means we have permission to proceed into the next section, and at 11.10 we're given the 'right away'. No. 7714 starts off in full forward gear, and once we've got the train moving she's brought back to 35 per cent. Mike deposits eight shovelfuls all around the fire, keeping it thick under the door and around the sides, creating a saucer-shaped fire. We're running at about 20 mph. It's downhill from here, so Dave shuts her off and puts the blower on (to keep the fire drawing) and lets her roll into the dip at the bottom before opening her up again on the up-grade, on the approach to Country Park – a request-only stop, which is popular with some residents as it is closer to some parts of Highley than Highley station proper. The halt is on the site of the former Alveley Colliery, which was sunk in the 1930s. Because the colliery was on the other side of the river to the railway and the coal sidings, coal was initially brought over the river using a rope-worked tramway, which was replaced by an overhead aerial ropeway in 1961. The colliery closed in 1969 as it was uneconomic to work, and freight traffic ceased on the line (passenger traffic having ended in 1963).

We slow to 15 mph round the curve; the feed is put on and steam is shut off just before the summit. There is a red signal approaching, but it changes to green, giving us an all clear as we run into Highley. On the run into Highley is a Fixed Distant, which always shows caution/yellow to check the speed of trains approaching the Home signal, which, because of the Fixed Distant, is always presumed to be 'On' until seen as otherwise. We roll in on time at 11.18.

The village of Highley and its coal mines are among the reasons that the Severn Valley Railway was first built in the 1860s, and indeed account for its sinuous course along the valley floor. Highley is first mentioned in the Domesday Book, and coal mining and quarrying began in the Middle Ages. A blast furnace, fed with local coal that was transported on a horse-worked tramway, was in existence in the eighteenth century. The first large-scale colliery was Stanley Colliery (1804–23), on a site roughly where the station stands today. Spoil tips and earthworks stand witness to it. Billingsley Colliery opened in 1801, and the arrival of the railway led to a rapid expansion in coal mining in the 1870s. Highley Colliery started working in 1878 and Kinlet in the 1890s. Both Billingsley and Kinlet collieries had private branch lines, the Kinlet line being worked by a small 0-4-0 saddle tank, built by Andrew Barclay as works No. 782 of 1896, which is now preserved at Ironbridge Gorge Museum. Coal from Highley Colliery was brought down to the railway via an incline plane to extensive sidings at Highley station, where the Engine House Museum now stands.

Above: Highley station exists almost in a time warp, and exudes GWR atmosphere. (Gareth C. Price)

Left: The signal box at Highley is an original GWR box, built by Mackenzie & Holland in 1883. (Gareth C. Price)

A demonstration goods train is looped at Highley, in No. 2 siding. (Gareth C. Price)

The Engine House Museum at Highley, which houses several 'out of ticket' locomotives, stands on the site of the old Highley colliery sidings.

Return of PRIVILEGE TICKET ORDERS issued

(435)   Month of _July._ 189*3*.

| This Return must be filled in and sent to the Head of Department on the first day of each month. |

Waterlow and Sons Limited, Printers, London Wall, London.

Date.	No. of Order.	Applicant. Name.	Description.	Order in favour of	From	To	No. of Tickets issued.	Class (state whether Single or Return.)
July 1	44	W. Cole	Stn. Inspect	Self	Highley	Churchill	1	3rd Rtn
" 4	45	"	"	Wife (Daughter)	Kidder	Heath	1	" "
" 1	46	H. Powell	Signalman	Wife	Highley	B'mouth	1	" "
" 8	47	W. Cole	Stn. Inspect	Wife	"	Kidder	1	" "
" 5	48	H. Powell	Signalman	Wife	"	B'ham	1	" "
" 10	49	W. Cole	Stn. Inspect	Son	"	Bewdley	1	" "
3 " 15	50	H. Powell	Signalman	Wife	"	Kidder	1	" "
" 11	51	W. Cole	Stn. Inspect	"	"	"	1	" "
" "	52	"	"	Son	"	B'mouth	1	" "
" 22	53	H. Powell	Signalman	Self	"	Bewdley	1	" "
" "	54	"	"	Wife	"	B'mouth	1	" "
" 27	55	W. Cole	Stn. Inspect	"	"	Kidder	1	" "

Most railway companies granted 'Privilege Passes' to their employees, which granted them free travel, albeit in third class.

Highley station exists almost in a time warp, with only the original footbridge having been lost (in the 1970s) and replaced by the present structure in 2009. It is the only station proper on the SVR to have only a single platform face. The Engine House Museum, which opened in 2008, houses several 'out of ticket' locomotives and some on loan from the National Collection, as well as wagons (including one in the colours of the Highley Mining Company) and coaches.

Highley–Arley–Bewdley

Having made the appropriate token exchange, No. 7714 chatters away from Highley at 11.20. Due to the legacy of coal mining, there are lots of niggly speed restrictions in the area due to mining subsidence. There are also several ungated level crossings: both whistles are sounded as we approach to given any motorist due warning.

The River Severn is on our left as we sweep round the curve to Arley, and we cross the County Boundary from Shropshire to Worcestershire. The feed is put on as we approach, and Mike puts seven shovelfuls around the firebox. We arrive at 11.28. Arley is another time warp station, as only the LNWR signal box (recovered by the preservations from Yorton) can be said to spoil the GWR ambience. The atmosphere at Arley has led to it being used as several television and film locations, including in the BBC sitcom *Oh! Dr Beeching*

An Edwardian view of Arley station, which is perhaps one of the most atmospheric on the whole line.

Above left: Running into Arley, past the signal box.

Above right: Arley station house, with the signalman on the platform ready to catch our token.

with the addition of a row of fake railway cottages. Arley boasts a small goods yard, and in the 1930s it was home to a GWR camping coach for holidaymakers.

Arley has two platform faces and has the facility to pass trains. The original passing loop was removed in the 1960s by BR when the line became freight only, but it was reinstated in 1975 by the preservationists. As we are on a hill, Dave holds the train on the vacuum, and we get the 'right away' at 11.34, the guard giving us the top as the Home was already 'Off' when we arrived. We're due at Bewdley at 11.49.

Bewdley–Kidderminster

With the 'right away', we bark away from Arley, the exhaust echoing back from the soot-encrusted arch of the station bridge. The line follows the course of the river, sweeping in a sinuous reverse curve. We slow to 15 mph to cross over the Severn by means of the Victoria Bridge, which at 200 feet (61 metres) was the longest cast-iron railway bridge in Britain at the time of its construction. It was designed by Sir John Fowler, the original Chief Engineer of the SVR, and constructed by the famous railway contractors Samuel Morton Peto and Edward Brassey. The ironwork was fabricated at Coalbrookdale and the foundation stone for the bridge was laid in November 1859. Together with the rest of the line, it opened in February 1862.

No. 7714 accelerates away; we charge through the tree-lined cutting at Timperley, with the reservoir and sailing club on our right. Mike puts more coal on as we sweep past. The line

A Victorian postcard of the Victoria Bridge, which carries the railway over the Severn just south of Arley.

Rumbling over the murky waters of the Severn.

curves to the right, past the reservoir, and over on our right is the aqueduct that carries the Elan Valley pipeline, which supplies drinking water, entirely by gravity, from Wales to Birmingham. The railway follows the course of the river, which flows lazily on our right. Coming up is Northwood Halt, a request-only stop that is much used by residents shopping in Kidderminster. The Halt is rapidly followed by a concealed crossing. We slow to 10 mph and sound the whistle; despite this, we know that some drivers take their chances and try to cut across in front of an approaching train. Dave shuts off and lets her roll; Mike keeps a look-out and reports path clear, we've a clear road ahead. We roll through and open up after the crossing. She barks away uphill. Keeping his eye on the boiler pressure gauge, Mike puts seven shovelfuls of coal on the fire and washes down the footplate with slacker pipe to keep down the dust. Ahead is the Distant controlling the approach to Bewdley; it's 'Off', meaning that all the signals are clear, giving a clear run into the platform. The feed is put on and the site of the bridge that carried the former branch line to the Welsh Borders can be seen on the right. This was the old Tenbury & Bewdley Railway which opened in 1864 (two years after the SVR), which branched off the SVR about a mile north of Bewdley and ran on a parallel course before swinging off and crossing the Severn over the now partially dismantled Dowles Bridge.

73576.

Dowles Bridge, Bewdley.

Above: An early postcard showing the now partially dismantled Dowles Bridge, which carried the old Tenbury & Bewdley Railway.

Left: Tom leans over the cab side to hand over the token at Bewdley North Box.

The token is dropped at Bewdley North Box as we roll into Bewdley over the Wribbenhall Viaduct at 11.46. Beneath us is the lovely Georgian town of Bewdley (named from the French 'beau lieu', meaning beautiful place), which was, in the medieval period, a port on the Severn. Here we have a four-minute wait.

Bewdley is one of the largest stations on the SVR; it was formerly a junction and as a result has three platform faces. It is controlled by two signal boxes at the north and south ends of the station. The double track section of line between Bewdley North and Bewdley South is worked at 'Absolute Block' and can also be worked bi-directionally. The through line on Platform 3 is worked with 'Acceptance Lever'.

An Edwardian postcard of Bewdley station with a GWR steam railmotor drawn up at Platform 3.

No. 7714 basking in the sun at Bewdley, waiting for trains to cross.

Above left: A fireman's view of the run into Bewdley over the Wribbenhall Viaduct. The Georgian town is spread out below us.

Above right: Looking south, toward the water crane and Bewdley South Box.

Bradley Manor on-shed at Bewdley MPD.

The train we've been waiting for, a Peak Class diesel with the LNER teak set.

The final section of line (Bewdley–Kidderminster) is worked via 'Acceptance Lever' rather than token, so we don't have a token to exchange, but we still need permission to enter the next single line section. We depart Bewdley at 11.50 at a sedate 10 mph, passing the south signal box and traversing the viaduct, crossing over the Severn once more. From here on it's uphill all the way to the tunnel, so Mike puts eight more shovelfuls of coal into the glowing heart of No. 7714. On our left, African elephants and rhinos at the West Midlands Safari Park regard us nonchalantly. In the distance, we can see the old bridge that carried the line to Stourport and Hartlebury. Passing the former airfield, Mike puts on another round of coal.

As we approach the 480-yard-long Bewdley Tunnel, Dave sounds the whistle and puts the blower on before we plunge into the darkness. The blower is on hard to prevent something known as 'blow back', whereby the fire can enter the engine cab due to insufficient draught from the chimney caused by the limited clearance in a tunnel, or if the engine slips. Sparks cascade from No. 7714's chimney like a Roman candle, dancing past the cab spectacles; the only illumination in the cab is the glow from the fire. We pass the tunnel at line speed (25 mph) and burst into the sunlight, whistle screaming. Having breasted the summit,

Above: The bridge that carried the line to Stourport can just be glimpsed through the trees.

Left: No. 7714's whistle screams before we plunge into Bewdley Tunnel.

Above left: Sometimes the light that's at the end of the tunnel is the glow from the firebox.

Above right: Driver's eye view of the approach to Kidderminster Town.

Right: Running past Kidderminster Town Signal Box, which was built between July and December 1986, and commissioned in 1987 as part of a major re-signalling programme.

Above left: The GWR goods shed, part of the original station complex at Kidderminster, now houses the Kidderminster Railway Museum.

Above right: We've arrived: No. 7714 stands at Platform 1 in Kidderminster Town.

it's downhill all the way to Falling Sands Viaduct, which crosses the River Stour and the Staffordshire & Worcestershire Canal. We pass from the Severn to the Stour Valley and from here it's now uphill to Kidderminster. The scenery changes from open fields and woodland to back gardens and all the signs of a busy town, and in order to stay friendly with our neighbours we need to control the emission of smoke, especially as some houses have been built since the railway was re-opened. There's a speed limit of 15 mph as we make our approach to Kidderminster, passing the carriage shed and the diesel depot on our left and the main line station and carriage works on our right. We arrive at Platform 1 at 12.05.

Kidderminster Town is the southern terminus of the SVR and is built in what was the old goods yard – the original GWR goods shed now being home to Kidderminster Railway Museum. The main terminal buildings, despite their appearances, were built by preservationists. Kidderminster re-opened in 1984 (the earlier terminus being Bewdley), following the purchase of the old goods yard in 1982. It is a close copy of the buildings that formerly stood at Ross-on-Wye, and many visitors are fooled into thinking it is the original Kidderminster station. At first, the facilities were very primitive, with nothing more than a converted coach and a somewhat flimsy timber shelter. The present building was erected in three phases from 1984 to 2006. It is a typical mid-Victorian GWR station building, including lovely cast ironwork on the roof and a *porte cochère* entrance. It consists of a main entrance block and two wings forming a spacious concourse roofed over with an elegant glass and iron roof. The carriage shed is a fifth of a mile long and can house fifty-six bogey vehicles. It opened in 2000.

We uncouple from the train and run round, and take in water ready for our return to Bridgnorth. It's a glorious early summer day, and we grab some respite from the heat of the cab through eating an ice cream cone and sipping a much-needed cup of tea. Sitting on a platform bench alongside No. 7714 is another opportunity to chat to inquisitive members of the public, as well as reminisce about the days of steam. On one occasion at Manchester I got chatting with a very knowledgeable, rather elderly lady and her daughter. She knew all about lap and lead and notching up; over the course of the conversation it transpired that the lady's husband had been a driver on the LMS, and had driven the 'Coronation Scot' before the Second World War. During their courting days, he had often picked up his then fiancée at Crewe and she travelled with him on the footplate as far as Carlisle, and, as she said, 'You pick up a thing or two when your husband is an engine driver.' Completely against regulations of course, but love found a way. On another occasion, a very self-important lad proudly informed the crew of *Planet,* 'You can't burn rocks you know.' Puzzled expressions all round. 'You can't burn rocks', he repeated, pointing to the black stuff in the tender. Ah! Coal. He'd never seen coal before, so he didn't know what it was.

Our sojourn at Kidderminster is interrupted by the arrival of a very large, very blue, very noisy interloper – a Deltic. 'Quick! It's ruining the holiday. Let's go before we catch something,' remarks Mike as we depart Kidderminster at 12.56.

The station house at Kidderminster Town is an authentic recreation of a typical Victorian GWR station, and was completed in 2006.

Above and below: The recreated booking hall and spacious concourse, with its glass and iron roof.

Tom uncouples No. 7714 so we can run round and take on water.

Left and below: Tom clambers onto the tank tops to open the filler, while Mike swings the arm over and opens the water valve to top up the 1,200-gallon tanks.

Right: We've run round and coupled up, and the white head lamp is fixed to the bracket in the middle of the bunker, signifying Class B or 'Ordinary Passenger Train'.

Below: The fire has been allowed to run down while we've been standing ...

 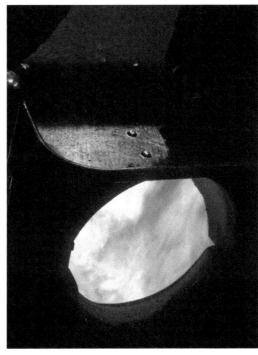

Above left and right: ... but Mike very quickly brings it round.

Below: A very large, very blue, very noisy interloper!

Kidderminster–Bridgnorth

On the return leg, Dave and Mike change places so Mike takes over the regulator and Dave the shovel. As we drift out of Kidderminster Town, the fireman looks back to make sure every carriage is coupled up (and following us) and that no doors are open. We roll down the hill to the Section Signal, and with permission to proceed Mike opens her up to 20 mph to the viaduct. As we're running bunker first, coal dust from the bunker becomes a problem so Dave puts on the feed and uses the slacker pipe to spray down the coal and footplate. The doors on the rear cab sheet are opened to let in some much-needed cool air, but it brings with it more dust from the bunker. Because the coil-sprung wheelset are now leading (running bunker first), No. 7714 is far more bouncy. She bounces over every rail joint, the coil springs clashing and clattering against their covers. Dave puts coal on before Bewdley and the yellow distant changes to green, signalling our approach. We've got green all the way in and drift into Bewdley at 13.07, where we have a two-minute wait. We pick up the token for the next section and depart at 13.10. With an ungated crossing coming up, we slow to 10 mph and give one long blast on the whistle. The crossing lights show white – it's all clear – and we proceed cautiously over.

Fireman's view of the signal gantry at Kidderminster as we clatter through the pointwork, heading back toward Bridgnorth.

Left: A portrait of a happy man: Mike takes the regulator of No. 7714.

Below: Crossing over the Falling Sands Viaduct, which spans the River Stour and the Staffordshire & Worcestershire Canal.

Above left: The southern portal of Bewdley Tunnel

Above right: Running bunker-first into Bewdley, where we cross No. 1501 and her train for the second time.

At Northwood Halt we pause to set down passengers and make our run into Arley at 13.21. Dave lets the pressure drop on the approach so that we don't blow off in the station. He can build the pressure back up before we depart (13.25). We arrive at Highley at 13.34 and have a three-minute wait, so the opportunity is taken to put on the feed and build up the fire. It's an uphill start from here, and No. 7714 barks away in full reverse gear, the reverser handle jumping in the quadrant. Dave remarks that a Bulleid Pacific would struggle here, and slip on the bank, but No. 7714 just romps away with her load of six carriages in tow. He also notes that a Bulleid in need of some tender loving care would use 3,500 gallons of water and 3 tons of coal on a return trip from Bridgnorth to Kidderminster and back – No. 7714 won't use that amount in a day and will still do the same amount of work. Then again, it's a case of 'horses for courses', as they were designed for running at a continuous speed on a more or less level road, rather than working a country branch line.

A two-minute stop is made at Country Park and from here we can roll all the way to Hampton Loade; we get green signals all the way through. We arrive at 13.45 and tokens are exchanged. The feed is put on and we depart at 13.50. We charge up the 2 miles of the 1 in 100 Eardington Bank, the cab of No. 7714 bouncing and swaying, exhaust barking away, with 190 psi in the boiler and the needle on the gauge flicking as the engine works hard. Mike shuts off just shy of the summit and we arrive in Bridgnorth five minutes early at 14.00. We've a fifty-minute layover here to take on water and grab something to eat and drink before making our second round-trip to Kidderminster (departing Bridgnorth at 14.45 and arriving at Kidderminster at 16.00) and back (departing Kidderminster at 16.55).

Above: The typical GWR 'Pagoda style' shelter at Northwood Halt was built in 2006, replacing an earlier wooden hut.

Below and opposite above: No. 7714 scampers along with her passenger train through countryside in bud and bloom.

With Mike driving, it's Dave's turn on the shovel.

Above: Slacking-down the footplate to dampen down dust.

Below: Catching another breather at Hampton Loade.

Mike takes the coal pick into the bunker to bring some coal forward. It was full this morning.

Chapter 4

Disposal

We run bunker-first into Bridgnorth, just as the parish church clock has finished striking 6 o'clock. We uncouple and run round the carriages so we can enter the yard and proceed to our stabling point for disposal. Disposal is quicker than prepping an engine, and can be a lot dirtier. On many steam sheds, just as there were steam raisers (who lit the fire) there were 'fire droppers', whose job it was to either clean the fire in between runs using the curved pricker and clinker shovel, or to drop the fire. They did this by either raking the fire through the bars into the ashpan, or by bailing it out using the clinker shovel. On a tender engine, the handling and manipulating of these long, heavy, pieces of iron is *relatively* easy, but in the confines of the cab of a small tank engine like No. 7714 it can be difficult, and indeed dangerous. Not all sheds had fire droppers or wet pits:

At Gorton, if you came in from the main line on steam, and got over the wet pit, opposite Priory Signal Box, you had fire-droppers to do the disposal and drop the fire for you. We'd come in over the wet pit, and report to the supervisor and find whether the engine needed turning. There was a cabin for the foreman where there was a large chalkboard and we'd read which of the twenty odd roads we'd been put on.

If you were on a fire dropping turn, you would have about eight engines and you could get them done in a short time, and then book off and away you went, or you could take your time, go for a pint, come back and do another.

Disposal at Newton Heath depot in the 1960s followed a similar pattern:

At Newton Heath, when you came in off a job, you had to do all the work yourself. First, you'd go under the coal hopper and fill the tender. The engine was watered, too. There was no wet pit and you had to drop the fire yourself. We'd take four or six fire bars out under the door with the big pinchers, get the rake and drop most of the fire through in to the ashpan, and then rake out the ashpan. You had to be careful of the brick arch. We just kept the fire in under the firehole door, just to keep enough steam for the brakes. If there was not enough steam, the vacuum wouldn't work: you needed twenty or twenty-one inches

A master of his craft: Dave brings No. 7714 into Bridgnorth on the final trip of the day.

vacuum on the small ejector, and so long as you had enough steam for the small ejector you were all right. But, you could make the vacuum brake into a steam brake, by lifting a clip on the ejector, so if you don't have enough steam, you use your rag and just pull the little plunger out to get the brake to go on.

We'd go down to the cabin and the engine was booked in; we'd see on the big board what the engine was to do for the next twenty-four hours, if it was to get attention from the fitters, go straight back out, or told if the engine wanted turning: 'Head up' meant it was facing to Yorkshire and 'Head Down' toward Manchester. The engine was got ready for the next job. We collected our tools and took them back to stores, for the next lot of men.

Turning an engine at Leeds led to one misadventure:

We used to go into Leeds City, coming off Platform 16 at Manchester Victoria with the afternoon perishable from Blackpool. We'd come off Newton Heath, shackle on, and take it into Leeds City. At Leeds we'd hook off and go on the turn table to turn the engine and then go back to Leeds Central. We'd go back to Manchester with the early morning 'Ghost Train' back to Victoria.

On this one occasion, we went into Leeds City and went to turn the engine, except that the fireman missed the road by about four inches. He'd fetched one of the levers at the end of the turn table over too quick, and had missed the road. The lever missed the plate and got stuck in the wall. Well, we couldn't get off, so we had to go to Leeds City and get help from their staff, but it was getting on for midnight so there weren't many men about, so the engine was stuck there. We told control what had happened. We were told to shut down the engine – make sure there was enough water in the boiler, bank the fire, and secure it – and then were sent over to Holbeck Loco to pick up an engine and take the train on to Manchester with a Leeds engine. When we got to Manchester no one was any the wiser. We just booked off as usual and left the engine – it was down to control to get it back to Leeds!

The job of dropping the fire of No. 7714 is made easier because she is fitted with both a rocking grate and a hopper ashpan. Both of these are preservation modifications. Instead of traditional cast-iron fire bars, a rocking grate has a grate made from a series of cast-iron sections that can be rocked using operating gear in the cab. The grate is divided into front and back sections, which can initially be operated with a limited range of movement so as to break up any clinker that may have formed when running; alternatively, they can be rocked fully to enable the fire to be dropped. A hopper ashpan, unlike a standard 'flat' ashpan, has hopper doors on the bottom and is a labour saving device 'to facilitate the disposal of the fire'. The doors can be opened using an operating lever, and should be opened before the grate is rocked, so as not to drop burning coal and embers into the ashpan. With a normal ashpan, the ash has to be raked out using a long T-shaped ash rake, usually into a pit beneath the engine. It is hard, filthy work, especially if the wind is in the wrong direction.

The blower is put on to stop flames, ashes and dust entering the cab. With the hopper ashpan doors open, Dave uses the fire irons to rake through as much of the fire as possible before shaking the grate to break up any clinker, and then finally rocking the grate fully

Shrouded in steam from her drain cocks, No. 7714 back on shed after a long day.

A selection of fireman's tools, including clinker shovels, darts, prickers, rakes, and even a long-handled frying pan for the all-important breakfast fry-up.

Having opened the hopper ashpan, Tom damps down the ashes with the hose. This cools the ashes and helps reduce dust.

Dave uses the fire-irons to riddle as much of the fire as possible through the grate into the ashpan.

Above left and right: The grate is rocked using the operating gear in the cab, first to the 'shake' position to clear any clinker, and then fully rocked to dispose of the fire.

Left: The grate is clear apart from a small warming fire, which will be left overnight.

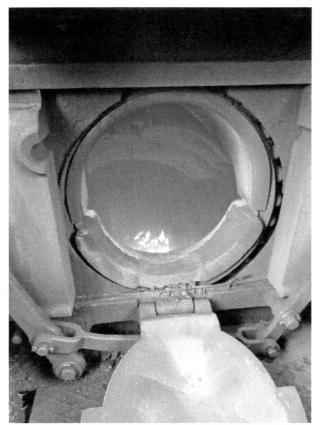

to dump the hot coals and embers into the ash pile. A hose pipe is used to dose down the hot ashes and also to keep down dust that could enter moving parts and bearing surfaces.

Not all of the fire is disposed of: some clean fire is usually left on the grate overnight to keep the boiler warm, and thus lessen warming up stresses/expansion on the boiler the next morning. If the locomotive is not in service the next day, a small warming fire is still left in to give a slower cooling cycle, so that the boiler cools more slowly, which is better for the lifespan of the boiler.

While the engine is standing over the pit, the injectors are put on to fill the boiler almost to the brim ('to the top nut') to ensure that the boiler is full for lighting-up in the morning. Because water expands as it gets hot, even if the boiler is filled right up at disposal in the evening, the water level will have dropped by the morning as the boiler has cooled down. This is why it's important to get as much water in the boiler as possible, as the only way to get water into the boiler is using the injectors and these rely on boiler pressure to operate them. If the water level is too low, the boiler can be backfilled by using a hosepipe up the injector overflow, or by a fitter removing a wash-out plug. But this is to be avoided as it puts cold water directly into the boiler, which leads to larger temperature changes within the boiler, and because the cold water has lowered the temperature of the boiler, means it will take longer to raise steam. Where a locomotive does have a feed pump (usually driven off the cross-head), like the replica of *Planet*, it can be shunted up and down by the yard shunter to put water back into the boiler that way.

Mike goes round to check the bearings of the coupling rods, using the back of his hand to test their temperature to see if any have run hot, and does a quick inspection underneath.

Happy that the boiler is full, that the engine is secure (hand brake screwed on; regulator closed; engine in mid-gear; drain cocks open) and that a small warming fire has been left in overnight, we can complete any paperwork, and book off at the end of the day, a job well done. We're tired and dirty, but happy. It's been a twelve-hour day; we wash up (and enjoy one luxury unknown in steam days: a hot shower), and head to the pub for a well-deserved pint and a meal.

Stepping onto a locomotive footplate is more than just about nostalgia; none of today's crew remember main line steam. My own first recollection of steam was travelling behind *City of Wells* on the Worth Valley and regular summer trips to the North Yorkshire Moors in the late 1980s. There is an allure to steam, a sense of wonder; it's often been said that the steam locomotive is the closest mankind has yet come to creating artificial life. Those of us on the footplate, the fitters, cleaners, boiler makers and painters are keeping history and skills alive for future generations; or, with replica locomotives like *Planet,* re-learning lost skills. There is a deep sense of tradition, of pride in the job, that we are part of a family of drivers and firemen which stretches back two centuries to the time of George Stephenson. But moreover, we do it because we enjoy it: it's fun, it's hard work and it's dirty work, but there is nothing as exciting as being on the footplate of a steam locomotive working hard or running at speed. There is a deep sense of satisfaction from having spent the day with like-minded colleagues on the footplate, and having given members of the public an enjoyable day out; having rekindled memories in an older generation, and inspired the next.

> 'For two years I remained with the *Rocket*, working her and getting to understand her in every part – and to love her, as if it were a human being, just as I love her still and always shall.' – Edward Entwistle, driver of the *Rocket*.

Left and below: Mike closes the hopper ashpan and the engine is moved over the pit; the pile of ashes gets a good dousing.

Back where we began over twelve hours ago: boiler full and warming fire in, ready for tomorrow's turn of duty.

Acknowledgements

I would like to thank the Severn Valley Railway, and in particular Dave Ward, Mike Ward, and Tom Mills for their hospitality and a chance to spend the day shadowing them on the footplate, and also for their checking of this manuscript. Thanks are also due to Adrian Bailey for sharing his reminiscences of his time on main line steam in the 1960s; Gareth C. Price for use of his photographs; and Andrew Mason for his excellent graphics, and proof-reading.